Books by Roy Morrison

We Build the Road as we Travel: Mondragon, a Cooperative Social System (Essential Book Publishers)

Ecological Democracy

Ecological Investigations
(Forthcoming from Glad Day Books)

The Loggers of Warner

Roy Morrison

A Glad Day Book

Warner, New Hampshire

Copyright © 1999 by Roy Morrison

All rights reserved. To reprint, reproduce, or transmit, in print, electronically, or by recordings, all or part of *The Loggers of Warner,* beyond brief excerpts used in reviews, please contact the publisher for permission:

Glad Day Books
PO Box 114
Warner, NH 03278

ISBN 0-9658903-1-7

First Glad Day Books edition, 1999

Second printing, May 1999

Printed in the United States of America on partially recycled paper by R. C. Brayshaw & Co., Warner, New Hampshire.

Cover design by Adam Auster.
Photographs by Roy Morrison.

Orders: 1-888-874-6904

www.essentialbooks.com

The Lord shall record when he registers the peoples, that this man was born there. (Sela) And singers and dancers alike shall say; All my springs are in there. Amen.
Psalm 87, (6-7).

Contents

AUTHOR'S NOTE 11

BOOK I
Spring: Gatherings 13

BOOK II
Summer: Toward the Harvest 41

BOOK III
Fall: Grey Rage Lightening 69

SAMUEL 85

EPILOG 89

Photographs

Woods, Northern New Hampshire	17
Doug Newton with Logging Pick on Newmarket Road	21
Sunflower in Our Garden 1997	23
Truck Back to the Land	27
Jennifer Ohler with her Horse	31
Tractor Drive Wheel	33
Doug's Wood Conveyor	39
Peter Ladd Repairing Barn Foundation	43
Rock Shadows Contoocook	47
Bob Bower Fixing Skidder	51
Log in A Sandpit In Contoocook	53
Doug's Tractor Wheel	57
Pepper Basket	67
Pine-Shingle Pile	71
Post for Barn	75
Pigs	81
Winter Trees 1997	84
Sam and Jan	93

Author's Note

This book's inspiration is my life in Warner, New Hampshire. While in many ways it is written in witness and in tribute to the life ways of my friends and neighbors, *The Loggers of Warner* is not meant as either documentary record or journalism. It is my narrow slice of Warner, and that taken only with the selective, introspective eye of poetry. I am well aware that this book as narrative does not begin to do justice to many of my neighbors who work in the woods, nor to the lives of the people of our town. *The Loggers of Warner* is inspired by the happenings of several months, whose reverberations, of course, resound with the store of my life's memories. I hope that my writing, at times, rises to reflect the sharp sparks of truth cast by the lives of my neighbors.

This book was shaped by the attentive comments of readers in Warner who read the manuscript in various incarnations. These include Maxine Kumin, George Packard, Doug Newton, and Peter Ladd. The shortcomings that persist are, of course, a reflection of the judgment of the writer and not the readers.

Friends and writers Robert Nichols, Grace Paley, Joel Kovel, and Jay Moore in our collaborative work helped bring the label of Glad Day Books to life and *The Loggers of Warner* to print.

I thank Adam Auster, who graciously designed both the book and cover, and the staff at R. C. Bradshaw for patiently helping to educate me in the mysteries of book production.

I

Spring:

IN DOUG'S DITCH
cut two feet wide
five feet deep
a hundred and twenty feet long
through loam, clay and hardpan *More An*
from house to garden to pigpen *Epic*
There's more an epic
than the silent volumes of
Barthes, Mumford and Polayni
piled waiting, leering
upon the couch.

By Doug's ditch
the scuffed rocks
yanked with iron bars
are laid dead
on the earth.

Eventide and
cool drops strike
a syncopated gong
from the blazed drip edge
Peter cobbled
along the roof
in his spider walk
three years ago.
A hundred feet in the air,
or crouched amidst the
guts of an engine,
Peter has time,

the presence to see
the bolt invisible joining
the world,
the odd singular tool
drawn from his belt
or his box to grab the
hidden spring, raise the
countersunk screw with the
stroke of Sonny Rollins
riding a sculpted note.

Spring here has almost no idiom
beyond turning, an explosion,
sucking breath away
to destiny, telos unleashed.
New Hampshire's spring is flattened,
winter eliding to summer.
Glottal stops of wonder
a blow to the head
after snow and frozen mud
then sweet pale greens swelling,
crescendos of swift glories.

The first no-seeums
have come with the night.
Nosing into my hand,
almost all wings with a round
tiny black head fit
for a welt-raising feast.
Escape is to turn off
the electric lights and hide
under percale sheets.

Old logs and
brown spiders on
rainy Sunday.
We feed and water
Doug's pigs.
The two largest wheel and
nose out the third
as we pour pale brown
pellets into their black bucket.

We settle and
pigs settle
into country domesticity
negotiating roles.
We carry and feed
they eat and be eaten.
Pigs are young,
porcine rotund
snouts moist expressive
snuffling, rooting, chewing.
Personalities and pigs thoughts,
passions more than beacon
desires and stratagems abundant.
This spring, long summer and
oblivious to our sense of
common purpose or not
the fall mercy of the butcher.

Sparky, the dog,
enamored, jams her
nose between the pen's
boards,touches their snouts,
reaches through with her
paw and taps them on their heads.
Excited, the pigs cry out keening
run in smart small circles.
Sparky loops around the pen
puts her legs up on the top rail.
She could easily
leap the fence, but hesitates.
Afraid of pig teeth?

Or dog's allegiance to people's lines?
Or memory of the pens
she lived in for a month
at the pound.
Advertised as pet of the week,
but unadopted, fierce in her picture,
the muscles in her strong
shepherd's chest tensed into planes
of frightened anguish.

We asked, Jan and me
for a bad dog. A smart dog
that needed rescuing.
Sparky loved spun
the pain of Sparky abandoned
to devotion. Riding in
the car between Jan and me,
she presses her head in loving
caution against the side of my face
if I raise my voice even in jest.
She named herself, chasing sparks
from a new year's bonfire.

Uncovering

The second rain day
and the tiny rose-colored
salamanders are arrayed along the woods track
striding off Newmarket Road, our road,
that slowly vanishes in a swale
of swamp maple and memory.
Picking up a salamander with
care, interest and arrogance,
returns me to the Catskills
forty years past
where I gathered them by the jarful.
The Catskills where we dug
worms from the farmer's
black writhing earth,
where the heroes were fabled
fisherman fathers at the bungalow
colony. The Catskills where

before Labor Day my girl
friend and I raided bungalows and
stole a softball, where I
saw my first Rosh ha-Shana service,
heard the shofar, remembered the
man with a tallis over his head,
hushed silence and mystery,
 a glowing dream and thought -
I think I did,
with curiosity,
a sense of wonder
and violation,
I was going,
a Jew was going into a church.
My Judaism then is the religion
of cities, of imposing Yeshivas,
busy streets lined with small stores
scattered diadems of synagogues,
Hasidim singular and rushing.
The Judaism of memory.
An ocean.

Here is the Judaism of
dew's silver baubles
on sunlit expansive mornings
emptied of people.
The Judaism of bears and white Christian
villages. The Judaism of identity.

Salamanders and shofars,
the perfect knitted waywardness
of the G-d nudged swirl of life.
Walking alone mixes memory
and duty rushing to conscience,
from the wood's implacable glories
to humanity's precincts,
to the Buchanan rally tomorrow
beginning the campaign next time.
And I, prodded by
conscience and identity,
must stand to bear the

threatening, mocking the scorn
and slurs and the face,
of my fear.
Can I poet and leaflet too?
Can I poet and write singing
prose truth that rouses itself
from the pit of lugubriousness,
that walks atop
the fence between ego
and action, boredom and clarity.
Rising toward truths
that parse identity as proud welcome
and not a spear.

NOW LET US SING THE
work-a-day heroism in
the woods of Doug and
Bob and Peter and Jennifer,
and Paul Hickie exiled *Heroism*
to the coast on a lobster boat.
The heroism of sure movements,
the repetitive ballet
of wood and steel and
greasy machine, of horse and
heavy chain and dirt and skidders
where logs are scaled
into dollars and life and
sound limb by the careful
enough grace that balances
effort with restraint in
the killing of the trees.

The logger's
dance is not just with
metal and wood but
between industry and country
between landscape and deathscape
between living earth renewing and
all the sad, hard dying.
When Bob Bower on his six hundred
Kearsarge Mountain acres,
upon whose wistful vista a clutch of
celebrated poets inspire -
When Bob Bower
with tree trunk arms sings of
his life as farmer and logger
he rolls for the earth
in bountiful battle against
gnawing paving counting
madness.

Is this truth of the
logger's dance,
guilty knowledge uncovering
a forbidden truth
to be smothered.
in death's raptures?
Memory in the stutter step
of the woods ballet
opens the door to revelation.
Memory, a double bitted ax.
One edge my maybe wisdom,
clarified as shiny butter,
by books and theories.
The other, pitted with
the burrs and caverns of the past
hiding guilty knowledge
reverberating through time's
stone-walled labyrinth,
my childhood sharp ecstasy
screaming and howling through
my forty-five year old mouth.

The country is twisted in
the jaws of the metal eaters,
pavers, tract housers, bankers
defining country
perched between wilderness and city.

When trees fall
in hazy countrytime it's
in confluence of noise
signifiers and the brute drop,
not conquest
but that rough respectful
return to balance,
to rutted skidder tracks
where mud puppies wallow,
but resplendent hillsides,
to the great great grandchild
the first trees fallen
to colonial axes again
sheltering trails of diffident
moose browsing.

Killing and Building,
where everyday acts
amidst violence and necessary grace
wear the patina of danger
and dreams and desperation,
the roars and tumults
singular silences
remind me
by trope and perhaps
bits of wisdom
that I too
am the logger.

Country
Cadence

POLE BEANS AND SQUASH HILLS PLANTED,
morning devotion to afternoon
exhaustion in work
rhythmed not factoried.
Winter squash along garden borders
edged with mulch spilling outward over
witch grass waiting and laughing,
boring with its tan rope roots weaving turf,
taking back black earth
from the worms beneath
fifty scattered hay bales.

Wooden poles, bought from Ted Young,
set between the squash hills.
Seven Kentucky Wonder seeds
plugged around them like Chiclets
smooth and shining
pressed into soft earth
swallowing fingers
to the border of my palms.
Past hay's boundary downhillside south
is Peter's second plot,
cross rototilled and seeded with buckwheat
leaping like school children from the earth,
waving flowers for hands.

Tomato plants
from Doug set out.
Hard hoeing in sodden soil where
fat worms have drilled deep.
I cut angular caverns for
early Cascade (no Jet Star this year),
plums, cherries, Nepals, Katahdin—
no, that's a potato—
caverns for the scoops of manure,
peat pot sides ripped
then put deep
tomatoes branches buried
to root strong.
I should have had a shovel.
Broad hoe and the trowel
makes shoulders ache.
I mourn for worms
I fear sliced by cruel
tomato cages rammed with
steel tripods into the earth.
I fling witch grass roots into
the border.

And Peas, glorious sweet peas
in June prevail.
Swelling gently
peas sweet as Jan's belly
Sweet pods in
bright green glowing
early summer sharp green bounty.
Peas piled atop spinach
and Black-seeded Simpson,
Ruby, Bib and Buttercrunch.
The white hearts of cauliflower
throb in green mantle.
Two young striped beetles
copulate on a potato leaf
I grab them and
flip them into the wind.

Snakes are living in the mulch hay
luxuriating under the blue tarp
lying in the sun atop the manure bag.
Cooing calm to writhing snakes
I grab Mimi's waxed paper
cold caps to sun dry them.
The top one off, and
the second and third caps explode
with tiny black ants that have
in a few days established
society between the paper's narrow channels.
Ants stalwarts hoisting huge
larva loads or hauling food packets
undaunted by my intervention.
I lay the ants back down to
recapitulate their culture and lives.
The next day, when I
return to plant,
all the ants and their baggage
have gone.

I practice the accounting of privilege,
of ant lives endangered
when I plant sodden
cosmos seeds and pat the soil gently down,
and ant lives spared.
Balancing guilt and remorse and redemption,
for license and permission as a dealmaker
to go onward.

To Bunker's Place

Green days in mosquito woods
slathered with sweat
from a Sunday birthday
hike, Jan and I cool in
the resplendent fancy
of a New London tavern.
New London of wealth
where the houses are old,
beams heavy and pegged
and the suffering visible
mostly in well-dressed faces
and Cheever pained souls.
What is felt, I conjecture,
amidst happy propriety
is a wistful grimace.

The June woods fill with
clouds of small mosquitoes swarming
after two rains.
We climb the Bunker trail off Pingree Road,
the fine Pingree farm restoring at our back.
The Bunker farmstead, wreckage now
in a high mountain meadow
stuffed with buttercups, bordered with violets,
lady's slippers hanging in the woods pendulous.
The buttercup meadows say love me

sweetly love me, make love with me,
but the mosquitoes
say feed me, and we
not lusted enough to test
their blood madness walk on.

Old Bunker they say carried his house
on his back two hundred years ago to
the meadow looking to the
Kearsarge Ridge southeast
with Mount Sunapee crouched
behind now tall trees northwest.

(Ted, the great Belgian
draft horse, skidded the supplies
for Peter's cabin up a snowy mountainside,
the sled bucking and bouncing over
rock, stump and deadfall.)

We're climbing in sweet, green spring woods
steep pitches, clouds of mosquitoes
Jan yells, "you'll carry the baby next year."
Suddenly a club moss blanket,
a cut in a stone wall
and idyll-smashing land raped ledges
clearcut in strips across the hillside,
gravely hammered,
as loggers say of cuts leaving
but a few seed trees and those
not yet marketable or worth chipping.

Even with New London's wealth
no illusion hidden one mile from
the Pleasant Road,
behind the sward of green
a hacked moonscape
with red trail blazes
pinioned to the survivors
along the logging road
bisecting and devastating the
Wolf Tree Trail of huge old
trees that swallowed sunlight
and water to shade the cows
of Old Bunker and his
Pleasant Street neighbor pioneers.
The deadwood lies gray, the
trunks parched, sapless, without sprouts—
the fate of the devastated
softwood forest on slender,
sandy upland soils.
What metaphor is needed?
A rape is a rape...

But through the curtain and into
the higher hills, the rocky juniper
groves above Bunker's paradise
where the old fifteen foot long cellar hole
still smiles amongst the buttercups.
On the peak thorn apples have grown
to half shade Sunapee Ridge
shimmering in the haze.

Web of Association

THE MOON HAS A CELEBRATORY CLARITY
face bright toward
the night in crisp June air.
The earth renewed in days
of grace and Peter's animal tales
A fawn, days old huddles in the grass
just outside the lower garden
as Peter mows. The deer, size
of a small dog or large cat,
in witch grass nursery,
protected only by silence
spots and tallgrass,
watches the mechanical
monster roar past
with deer poise, faith
and innocence.
Moose prints outside
Peter and Vicky's cabin, after moose
amble from hemlock groves
filing rocky glades
higher in the Mink Hills.
Trout in Peter's pond scooped from
narrowing August draught pools.
He flings small strips
of bologna and the
half-dozen trout rise to
strike the lunch meat
grab it, dark down
to be devoured
with fish pleasure.
Await on the
electric fence. The deer I
suppose, like dogs, are allowed
one bite.

World saver wouldbe I am daunted
by the weight descending
shocked by the respect of those
who seek direction from my chaos.
Eighteen months in the life
of We Build The Road
no rock star, but
author author
minor author expert professor,
Central American letters
Central Connecticut State University on Earth
Day, my Brooklyn alma mater,
and apotheosis, Harvard too.
Recondite recognition becomes request,
opportunity, the lubricity of fate
and circumstance.
But embarrassed by bad Spanish
that's proximate excuse to
stop my fraud being uncovered,
I say nothing to the proud and brave
Nicaraguans at Ash Eames' party
cooperators and musicians whose
accordion fills the light summer air
with strength, joy, confidence marching,
the courage *del barrio bajo*.
Ash, who understands, suggests gently
I can help with a partner whose
skills and vision complements mine.

Saver means worker
friend, co-celebrant
in life's dance,
not a master, a listener
who learns and then can teach.
In foibles folly,
savers deformed by ego
and the odor of cant
becomes savior,
a measure of divinity,
not humanity.

Chip Ferguson, friend of
Bob Bower in his
wild man drinking years,
when Bob cared for Chip's goat,
and kicked holes in the world,
upended tables, women and Harleys.
Chip's dad, Lou, met Bob and
was in fact friend, co-celebrant.
They walked together the first four hundred
Kearsarge Mountain acres
on an abandoned deadended road
that Bob would buy
to log and to live and to farm,
to marry fair and sturdy
Jennifer - mechanic, reader,
cordwood cutter, energy auditor -
a woman who throws mind
and body headlong to work to building—
and to two children, Abigail and Sam.

Jennifer, like Bob, child of
a doctor, the Ohlers of New London,
intimates of the Clevelands, James and Hillary,
Congressman, lawyer, Public Service Company
board member, citizens eminent responsible,
old Yankee New Londoners
Both doctor fathers released
from practice to good works.
Dr. Ohler building houses for the New
Hampshire poor with Jimmy Carter,
Dr. Bower traveling clinic worker for
Valdez, Alaska and once Soviet Union.

Lou Ferguson helped
balance Bob, equilibrated him
to the bank where he could
show a yearly board footage and cordwood
cut yielded a mortgage coverage sufficient.
Woods into dollars, woods into

a farm again on the southwest
edging to northwest side of
Kearsarge, the great mountain
that stares down at the Mink Hills
where I write.

"Six months ago I owned my farm,
now the bank does" Bob says about a
new small mortgage, and no health insurance.
But his sudden wild allergy to pine tree pollen,
the revenge of the trees, head squirting snot,
has past. Maybe release was allergy elixir,
or karmic re-alignment or another
grave factoid of clouded syncronicity.
Next year he'll chain saw his foot across
the arch, drive to the emergency room,
stitched he's again cutting cord wood in two
days.

Survivors here are not conquerors,
just the wilted and scabbed
weathered faces hanging on.
Survivors and relics inhabiting
a world simplified, as Bob Bower
survived on the banks of the
Contoocook River living in Lindbergh's
huge crate that shipped
the Spirit of St. Louis back from France.
Derelict, the crate lay on river's edge
for tramps, local heroes and sixties' hippies
to make separate peace.

Bob riding his Harley from
Contoocook River edge
to the Davisville tavern
to drink and watch the
knuckled hair-tearing
fights tumbling with
blood and curses into the dirt
into the snow
reddening.

Chip Ferguson, New Hampshireman,
is building a house on skids
from roughcut in Ash Eames'
land between house and pond
near the road.
On skids for Vermont escape
west across the Connecticut River,
thirty miles from the Wentworth Mountains,
to the convivial communities
of aging hippies in the Green Mountains
buzzing.
New Hampshireman practical, can build
a house on skids with wood butcher's skills
and sly enough Yankee grit.
On skids it's a
temporary building and not
tax appraiser's permanent improvement.
Like Alan Wagner's just down our road
a wood-shingled sugar house
store-bought combination windows
and shingles sliced by Doug's
19th Century shingle machine.
On skids to bring the sap
and sugaring to the customers
on a flatbed or to bring
the evaporator to the sap
on another sugarbush.
The sugar house built at the roadside
log landing where Alan and Doug worked
Alan's hillside woodlot.
Scores of great hemlock and pine for saw logs,
birch, beech and red maple for cordwood.
Oak when the price is right.
The sugar maples now largely alone
on the north slope,
to be drawn together by green
plastic sap tubing flooding
downhill with spring sun rising.

I worked with them one icy afternoon
of last year's snowless winter
(that'd be followed by this winter's blizzards).
Stopped on the way back from
Neale Carlson's sandpit to grit
the ice-covered walkways.
We kicked, pried and sledged apart
an ice-bound mountain of cordwood.
I tossed pieces to Doug
at the hydraulic splitter
ginned from the PTO,
the power take-off, of Doug's skidder.
The hydraulic ram pushing
a sharp wedge and the wood
rather quietly, inexorably parts.
We heave the split pieces
over our heads into Doug's large dump truck.
Its bending, prying, pulling,
tossing, hurling, the three of us
slipping and catching ourselves
on the greasy wood and
roughened ice in loggers' softshoe
and no nicks, only one or two
"watch outs." Thirty cords
will get you in shape says Doug.
Five hundred's a New Hampshireman's year,
but that's unsaid.
Five hundred's a pile twenty-four
by twenty-four by one hundred and ten feet
high. Life would be one mile of wood tall.

NANCY IS FILLING DOUG'S AND J.B.'S GREAT
ditch, the eighth wonder of Warner
piling shovelfuls of anonymous sandy earth
without fanfare on top of pipe and electric
cable
from house to pigpen.
The great ditch, logger's
testimony to days of strong backs,
men in sweat-crazed adventure,   *Quiet*
picks flying, iron bars pounding.   *Apotheosis*
Buried it's a tale
deeper, longer and wider
more resilient than mere work.
The pigs offer an opinion
as I dump rotten
vegetables into their bowl
they crunch the cantaloupe
and most of the rind,
chewing in the slops
with the determination matched by
the meat chickens who eat
faster than their legs can grow to support them.

Doug's purse is empty and
he is cutting oak on his hilltop woodlot.
Skidding great logs down the steep
that holds back the tractor
as a huge stabilizer. Without logs,
Doug stands on the brake
to slow the skidder as it dives.
Oak's two thousand dollars a truckload,
for the logger, at least four thousand and
maybe seven thousand for the mill.

II

Summer: Toward The Harvest

TODAY, HAMMERING ON THE SHOWER WALL
released, starburst, from the technological
cloud,
our child, say Sam, our
son Samuel Zohar
star brightness enlightened
star chromosomes normal
star floating in the warm
soft lake shining.
An exclamation punctuating
the tumult scurrying
that fills days,
masks contemplative refraction
raises the practical exceptions
that stuffs days with
convention stultification convention
cages years in blinding ritual.
What beyond my outsider's silence,
exile and cunning
can I give you my son?
How can I wrap you
in love instead of a blanket of
trinkets that transmutes
years to dross electronic?

Passages

Writer, I am boxed,
constrained by teenagers too
smart and the boredom of those
resigned to their fate
cursing silently
through gritted well-dressed teeth.
"In dingy light ... he felt himself
approaching a new dimension, one in which
he would have to live out the life he had
made."
writes Robert Stone, my novelist favorite,
another Brooklyn boy
artist manqué, now Connecticut-settled
boxed and celebrated laureate.
Writer, now it's sometimes
without bloody tears
that's felicity, or is it glimmers
of maturity, pain gritty pain run out.
Secret striver, boxes full of
poems unpublished unread, nipples unsucked
middle-aged joys.

Peter's life too is tossed up by
an offer from Belizian Reef
to teach scuba and escape
our glory's choking embrace.
For now he's gathering
lead mushrooms from snares on a
great boulder beneath New London's
Pleasant Lake. Peter's life
whose cadence is obligation
self-imposed, an accounting to square the
world with his discipline
to prod bloated circumstance
and a spoiled countryside
within the neon grasp
towards a balanced truce.
Resigned, almost, to

the blood of our country lives
running out despite pressure bands,
tourniquet, sutures,
the best of America dreams
Belizian dreams.

He's off on his Harley
selling diving adventures to Belize.
Peter shines with a recovered neatness,
New Hampshire roughness scraped away,
a scrubbed down discipline to uncover
a Lattimore English Public Schoolboy
in London waiting and dreaming
of Warner's woods.
Doug and Marge Ladd, 1950's
political expatriates by choice.
From Warner and
Paul Ladd, Sr.'s country store museum
to shops in Henniker and Main St. Warner
to Kensington antiquer.
Public schoolboy Peter
who horse logs, welds, rappels,
rides his bike up walls
and his tractor with brakes failed
down hillsides, firefights, dives,
roofs, shingles, mills,
reads, writes, thinks
public schoolboy. Knickers in a twist
Peter says, savoring a trenchant Englishism.
Shoeshine and a smile he calls
from the Harley. And when
they stop smiling back it's
an earthquake...
Peter's tuned his muffler
drilled holes sufficient to
capture a throaty
throb back off from a roar.
When he experimented,
riding downhill
a pealing clarion
rolled before him reverberating
in majestic anticipation.

Garden deers paid a karmic
favor, left a pile of scat signaling amidst
the potatoes, lettuce unmunched
I didn't turn on the electric fence
in praise of the baby deer
whose nursery was the tall
grass around the garden.
Respite is reasonably all expect.
Still, the fence stays off.
Mulch hay arriving Tuesday
potato beetles breeding,
but I leave the garden behind
to do vacation's bidding.

HERE'S THE CHANT OF ROY
not before the walls of Troy
but facing goldentop sun
waves whispering.
Facing the water *Vacation*
while punk kids downtown scowl
away from it barechested
longhaired and beautiful, trying
to be tough. One's shorthaired
smoking, ugly blue ink tattoos
dripped across his chest
with an ax-bladed iron cross
on right pecs, baby-faced,
smooth-cheeked, trying toughness
in a soft, soft pillow of a resort town
where cops a few years older,
stop to chat with homeboys
on the wall facing away from
whispering waves.

Nutcracking, I am reflective,
backed away from my book
to pry at what stands as
a predacious unity
our civilization unraveling in blazing
sun waves lapping.
Sun rolls down. The conquistadors return
from climbing Lafayette—
Jan's sister Nancy, and Dan just back
from Singapore, man, Singapore.

Peter's seaworld pulls me
a swimmer off Winnepesaukee dock
mask and snorkel and
the wonder of clear cold
northern waters, perch and
small bass hanging quietly
in the shallows among the
gray smooth boulders. I swim
face down in water womb time
along the shore
the lake bottom drops off
the precipice beckoning.
I glide over effluvia of
cables bottomed, tree limbs mouldering
in sun clear water,
a lake trout glowing.
A perch nosing up to me and we
float comfortable in silver water.
I glance right and left with my
snorkeled face, a Peter Ladd myrmidon.

My usual snorkel is confined,
repetitive as my usual hikes
 as if to swim or walk
too far is to awaken furies.

Later, a swirl onward reaching,
grasping bottom, breathing.
Farther in the glowing gloomy damp,
rain beating overhead
crayfish feeding from our hands
yearning forward pressing reaching
sunfish browsing rocks carousing
bubbling, Peter on my left.
The world tonight still scuba
world of invention exploration
intention, technique, rubber
suits, regulators, buoyancy vests,
many just so's to remember,
gauges harnesses and the cool
pressing rush of air compressed.
Weightless I am baby floating
in earth's water womb rolling

rising drifting up without effort,
and Peter lifts his hand
to drag me down.
Peter master diver trainer soon,
a deadly boy collection
of alliterative syllables.
Snorkeling's grace and writhing bodies,
scuba's life-on-the-line
equipment margin astronauticus.
Another forty-five new one.
Another proudly I wailed.

Looking for Torah in
Wolfeboro I find a Perot
supporter in his bookstore,
devotee of fast planes
and Washington corruption he
firsthanded. Not admitting
quickly as Perotista, but an
angry Republican with reminiscences
of wooden Gordon Humphrey and
smiling Bob Smith
Washington Senators damned Yankees
from New Jersey and Virginia.

Torah or Jesus
is bookstore scarce in this town
of many churches
somber WASPS
and resplendent Catholics
marching into Sunday's service.
But the Words'
only written outpost
seems the Christian Science Reading Room,
convivially on Main Street,
and given vacationers' wide berth.

Looking for Torah on Shabbat Eve
Tanakh in English left home in
vacation rush towards Jan's
family gathering. Near the
lapping Winnepesaukee waves.

Vacation's reopened gates of possibility,
future's entrance
for baby Samuel, headed
south from cabin fever February
racing stroller three-wheeled tripod
and now skin diving and dreaming.
Sail away.

A canoe glides with
the pace of sunlightened morning mist
in iconic outline
on Winnepesaukee waters,
voluptuous morning swim.
Red-crested woodpecker
large as a crow
beats on red pines
on a gray, mystical morning.
Across Winter Harbor
America roars.

NAMES CHILD NAMES
Samuel Zohar
ask G-d for him starbrightness
names, I think of

Hay Rides Ed Mary Rose Antes
pacifist light-footed continental walker
dancer smiling Mary Rose, the sacred balance
yin to yang beast to flower.
Ed with a pacifist
baby satyagraha waiting
to find her name.
Ed welcome friend who disappeared.

And soaring I am in the
haywagon dumptruck,
packaman of mulch.
Bob pitching sodden windrows
from a maybe bicentennial hillside field
oak bordered, for me to grape trample down.
The truck lurches
moving along rows
with a clang, pitching me
cautious, knees clutching hay,
into the steel frame.
In the fields
Bob hoists an orphan
bale water weighted,
over a hundred pounds sloshing
onto his shoulder from short right field
and hauls it to the truck
without a stagger,
thrusts it overhead.

Bob's playing men's hockey now
a geriatric team as
I'm geriatric poppa to be.
Once high school allstar and top scorer, again,
along the boards he elbowed a lawyer,
the New Hampshire Attorney General, and said,
"That's for the Clamshell Alliance."
And the AG didn't laugh.

Bob has the movie logger's
huge arms bear body
broad shoulders, thinning hair swirled.
His logger pants and tee shirt, like Doug's
are work-tattered from combat with
logs and heavy machines.
In the hay damp
I sway and roll with
the shifting contours of a field
now gathered beneath my feet.
Bob says, Seabrook used us up,
and I don't disagree.

SILENCE

Summer's Squalls and Graces

the country's silence
filled with the symphony
of leaves ruffling
wind dancing
staccato cries of chickadees,
warning chirps of chipmunks
beside their burrow,
squalls of cowbirds lofting
over Ted's shoulders,
buzzing of flies
green-eyed, lace-winged,
blood-sucking, nectar-drinking
birds' conversation on
riffling trees, rising to
spirited dialogue and argument.
Expectant sounds of a large animal in the woods,
the rasping flutter of swallows' wings,
I embraced country silence last year. I prepared
for jail for Seabrook civil disobedience
for sitting in Gov. Gregg's office.
I prepared for jail for isolation's terror alone,
stilled the radio, smothered the civilized
background noise that deafens minds
burying agonies personal
and common in torrents of
noise masking
the sound of hollyhocks singing.

Jail was not isolation and silence
but delousing showers and
cacophonous waves of sound
hoarse voices, clanging metal and
unspecified rasp of boredom.
Able to pay my way out,
I did and ran.

In the humid morning
air birdsong thick
mosquitoes swarm,
flowers rise up
a yellow rose has
opened and tiny wasps caress
dancing across sweet flower.
The chipmunks are eating
the Carpathian harebell at burrow's lips
and it's an emergency summer transplant.
Chipmunk dashes to stone wall
and Sparky's a spectator.
Poppies wave pastel orange sheets
in the breeze, inside they wear
purple blotches bolder than puce
that's the stamen's color and
six-armed anther riding
atop the green heart of
sweet dreams.
Behind the blue spikes of lupine's
angled flowers, ants cavort
around the pansies'
deep purple velour rims .
I stare into the flowers,
finding intimations of
Blake's universe.

Planting the potted
begonia and geranium
for summer basking
I unearth brown budding crocus bulbs snug
smooth and swelling
and press them back into
the soft wet brown earth
thinking of Sam our child voyager
in Jan's belly smooth soft warm.

Diving deeply
into mystery's warmth
we swam in flesh
measured pleasure's heights
rapture verdant glades
saw to one this
threeness, Jan and me
and Zohar brightness
little star is three.
Waiting for the baby
who moves with a glacier's
irresistible determination we
caress the surface carefully
and hope.

For Kim

SUDDENLY, KIM RADKE DEAD.
I've his presence vivid
in my mind
He's standing by a
 round wooden table on
an improbable valley back street
in Keene, New Hampshire.
A smile, gangly limbs long body
a shock of thinning hair
scooped at an angle
a man lost in
his own sadness it seemed
at a distance of bleak reports,
but together,
as spider-man etymologist
with a gracious edge
of the absurd,
he smiled.
On the floor in Oregon
dead, suddenly dead.
I hear the high modulated timbre,
the intelligence in your voice
gentle, reaching out
and pulling quickly back,
Kim dead.
A hole has opened up in the world.
I wish you peace.

DOUG DRIVING PAST WOODS BOUND
and I'm lying spinning moss bound,
flattened in July lushness
blanket of humidity and birdsong
windless sun dappling, *Rumbling*
leaves eager dancers *and Respite*
scarcely stir and grasses
hardly wave.
In hurried morning
Concord town I watched
a short-skirted woman dreaming
her concrete dreams.
Bear wrestled a clerk
at the Secretary of State's office.
Now moss-covered I lie as stone
on the Warner grass
buzzings, staunch imperatives
slipped into tomorrow.
Day roof fell down day
nay, but tumble down
day I lie.

The world that
was narrowed
overweighted with gloom
and dying,
not enough time,
is suddenly spacious,
a calm present textured with
tomorrow's allure swirling
as waving fields
calling calling.

Magical evening back
from Cambridge in the heat
An evening with fireflies
sailing on cool air flashing
as stars through the rising
pines where rain-swollen Slaughter Brook
roars accompaniment, and
Saturn with its yellow eye,
menace staunched,
swoons in the moon free sky.

In Cambridge good talk
anxious pleasures, in a land
of slimly requited agony.
Faces of punk children
with red and green hair and
jackets warning Amerika.
Cambridge cafe
That blonde woman
in the white dress knows
what smoking's all about.
She inhales deeply, thoughtfully with
conspicuous desire, feeling her
lungs fill and exhales
straight ample streams of smoke
to the side in a way
that's usually ugly and

ridiculous, but she's
mastered it and it suits
her angled, iconic and
scarcely labored beauty smoking
and Marlboros too.

FIRST RED TOMATO AND
green green basil
fan-size pumpkin leaves march
above the mulch
cabbage is heading   *Slaughter*
deer devour the snap bean tops   *and*
and buckwheat stragglers   *Apotheosis*
and volunteers from
Peter's covercrop.
Doug has two new rafts
of chickens penned in large
rectangular crates with
plywood bodies and
screen tops. The meat birds
swell to the size of petite
beach balls in weeks of frantic
eating. They balance on
scrawny legs, white feathers
pushed out in showy arrays.
Lifting up the screen
to feed and water,
the stench of chicken
is nauseating.
Skittish, they squawk, bounce
in a panic and begin
to pile on top of one another
until with soft voice
I calm them.

What do chickens think
of their destiny, of the meaning
and purpose of life? Are
there philosopher chickens
that debate the nature
of the grand beings
who provide food and water—
royalty, deity or ogre?
Does a chicken mystic
see fate in the freezer, and is reviled and
scoffed at by vituperative pecking brethren,
or do the chickens know
well their fate and by
chicken brains both reconcile
and transcend.

The males are slaughtered first.
Today or tomorrow Doug will cut two
arteries inside their mouths
and hang them inverted as
their life runs out
to chicken peace,
in chicken horror,
or realization.
He'll debrain them with a rod, scoop
out guts and leave them hanging to
be dry-plucked and frozen.
A few weeks later it will be the females.
"We're going to eat the chickens,"
says Ben, Doug and Nancy's sweet, strong
and smiling two-year-old.
"We're going to eat the pigs, too,"
he says smiling a country child
who knows where his meat and eggs
and vegetables come from.

He and them
we and they
there's no necessary calculus
of dispirited slaughter that
marches the killing man from

animals to soldier to
executioner?
There is blood precedent.
The farmer who kills
so that we may eat,
the soldier who kills
for survival and peace,
the executioner who kills by proxy
the helpless despised part of us—
That slouching, disorderly
poverty swarming, yelping
yapping, caftan-wrapped,
different child playful
kick
his face, my face
his face, kill him, kill her,
we and they,
us and them.

How can poetry
craft at truth
from horror and Shoah
by history
where the dead
are objects in agony.
The memory of slaughter breaking
the web of life, bleeding joy and bittersweet
alike.
Art somehow is necessary
not just for vowed neveragains
but to risk beyond
the weight of numbered cargo
photos of piled exhausted rictus corpses
recalling the humanity from
the house of screams.
Murdered dead are our families, neighbors,
friends, themselves, part of ourselves.

Executioners tire of pogroms
of slaughter in the farmyard
the measured reverberation of family
life screaming.
Executioners seek the shadow of camps
of killing machines to
slay not just mercilessly but
without passion.
Workaday factory killing
by accountants, by rote
killing that becomes stale
And knowing, having seen it not
just once, but again, again
still we march, close borders,
opine with fat faces about
aliens and national interest.

I, in Bosnia's desperation
was willing I said
to Jan, the Holocaust
ranting and rippling,
babies smiling tossed into the air
and bayoneted
I was willing
to bomb the camps
to kill the few
to save the many in a
quick executioner man's
trade, some for more
we for they,
but where
oh G-d, is peace.

Morning tide.
Guilt sits upon my head
as a big rock
crouching gray and mute
pressing a rock I hope that will vanish to
whispering vapors with
the sun rising.
Guilt with/without a face
my face/his face.

PETER EXULTANT, DOUG IN
his dumper hauling rocks
from Alan Wagner's woodlot road
to restful fill on Laddland
Doug's truck roars and belches *Waves of Joy*
diesel. I flash my garden *and Worry*
hose across his windshield to
celebrate his passing. The
truck hesitates as it climbs Howe Lane,
backs down, and shifting lower,
roars upward.

Peter's roaring
his elbow sprung and logging aches
to heft and split and haul
to hold the reins for hours
behind Ted skidding with fierce
aplomb. But Peter's roaring
with pensive exaltation,
happy Chief Diver Instructor man
now for Belizian lodge.
Diver, tourbooker, businessman
good fortune washes over him in
waves of joy and worry.

Doug pulling a hitch,
the sound thunders in
morning sun, eats air,
a beast sounding
without pause for breath,
and then the
symphony of the winds
closes in again.
The chainsaw screams
the sledge drives wooden
wedges, then a creak
a great crack
a tree plunging grasping
at surrounding branches
snapping, then the thud
the earth reverberating.
In the distance, Alan Wagner,
I suppose, bucks up the body
to cordwood size and the
sound is a faint whisper
annoying, mixing into the wind
floating with the rhythms of
country.

Wildlife,
sauntering in
Johnson's craggy brook my
feet grip mossy rocks
my legs are
waterstriders five feet wide.
Ahead the big culvert,
thirty feet of dark
sided mystery
brook and rocks flashing
at the end.

To do or to cower,
into the tunnel
and it's comfortable
beneath my feet,
the bumps on the side are rivets

not moiling spider caches.
Through and stepping
down into a four-foot deep
stream chasm,
then to a sandy beach.
Child's play for child dreaming
at forty-five.
Stream stalker rock wobbler.
My soles are
hardening.

Lightfoot on Little Sunapee
up strong on new legs and lungs
swinging on striped maple stalks
west ridge following west ridge
to rock ledge found then north
crab climbing rock faces
grasping pine shrub lifelines.
Sweat fogged, I'm on top,
on the rocks shrub-cloaked
and happy. Down southeast
lightfoot, I think, over
trunks off rocks and then
plunge through humus into a hole to
my knee. Lightfoot I'm balanced,
and then again along the stream
plunge into a hole that could have
snapped a wayward ankle.
Down wreathed with sweat
I dive into Sunapee
and lap swim bi-athlete.
I will pay tomorrow.

In morning time the broccoli
leaps into mist
heads after heads
side shoots, main shoots,
the russet potatoes lie in red clutches
beneath earth and mulch.
Tomatoes redden, crook-necked
squash explodes. Jan's belly
widens with our son, oh
our son. And I walking
toward or away from
madness lain footsteps
reverberating in the one
fine morning.

Owl calls in the rain
and fog shrouded night
who - who´ - who - who´
who - who´ - who - who´
four beats, twice

III

Fall: Gray Rage Lightening

SNOW TRACES
fly October first,
the air slaps our faces
a wet cold rag stinging while
maples blaze quotidian
crimson as fall plunges.
Jan is alive for two. The cold
is coarsening, toughening,
languor quickens her step.
Deer, fat and thickly coated,
move nervously in the cold.
Dreams wish would await
the smells of spring,
but Samuel's rushing at us
with the intensity of aeons and
sunrises. The midwife says
I can catch him in the birth bed.

A fall day another fall day
eighteen, nineteen years ago
the crisp sun cool
birds exclaiming enrapt
in the sounds of civilization.
Ground control to Major Tom
your circuit's dead
again. Eighteen years past a fall day.
The road crew's engines idling
as they maneuver the culvert.
Chipmunks a racket of exclamation

Autumnal Turning

and David Bowie, the oldies
show to shimmering memory,
the great white house on Ray Hill Road
of Wilmington, Vermont.
The fierce life-grasping of Kim,
Joan and Mary and Chris,
Brenda and Terry and Michael
and Roy. Sitting in that living room
an anthem of generational oddity,
and this living room remembering
before the great battle at Seabrook
and the long long retreat and parry
fighting fighting. Our anthems
are the sounds of civilization,
the song of the engine's roar.
Recovering in visions
of Samuel the aspiration
of possibility and prospect,
the exceptionalism of
the songs of voices
not engines.

James Richard Dunfey Ehrenberg
whirling in birth's exultation
to placid sleep in my arm's crook,
womb diving five day old,
a composed confident clarion welcome.
Root for the old Boston Braves
by Atlanta's proxy
to slake bonds of
Red Sox travail
I advise.

Bob's barnwarmer party in October
evening. Epic band Lunch At The Dump
arisen once more, who played at
Warner's Texas saloon whose
family of owners beat themselves
bloody in the snow as
fiddlers played, patrons cheered
and the beer flowed from the keg's open tap.
The grandmother was hell, Bob said,
with a frying pan she cracked bikers' skulls
with a cast iron thud.
The beers' non-alcoholic now
and fiddler's a carpenter,
though his eyes still dance.
An October cool country jam
with a log butt bonfire.

Traces and Survivors

SHOES SCATTERED ON THE
store carpet in vanity's
wake abandoned truly
deserted, left, not to
be clerk rescued but
resigned to ages by dust
impaled, entombed as
fossilized feet to be
snatched in a stone
millennial block for museum
display of our mysterious
antiquity.

Life rooms fled
before the SS Arrow Cross
Dinner settings abandoned
and recovered years
later, the same last
carrot morsel that slid
off the soup spoon, dry in
a dusty bowl.

Red squirrel boxed
on Newmarket Road
writhing, legs flying
eyes swollen tight.
Spared the shovel blow,
instead scooped to a
computer printer box, borne
to the vets scrabbling
against cardboard,
rescued, and that evening
alive.

Potatoes sleep cool
in their bins
abudding to wait the spring
their nights disturbed by
strange vegetable dreams of frying
and evisceration.

Dahlia and glad pried
clump troweled from
garden's faded blaze,
crouch on attic stairs in
a dark paper bag,
reserved bulb hearts
yearning to release
their bitter juices
climbing to exclamation.

Shoes reboxed
as if our son's potential
replaced, rewombed as
again. Commercial comings
repeat as life cannot.

My ego to mail's maw
to the publishers flail,
reappearing on inklines,
or just back, reject sorry sorry
in callous mystery thrown to the
hearth's capacious tomb.
My life to the womb
as I watch Sam
head down kicking kicking
my life my life my life.

              Peter off the planet
              on the reef
              with radio telephone lifeline
              On that occluded front,
Dividing   his partner Denny's back
              from the decompression chamber
              and spits at the risk of
              being paralyzed,
              blood bubbled to death
              And Peter, decentered
              in paradise worries.

Peter away has
traded endurance and stringency for
languor and endurance.
With snow he'd be trekking
to his cabin
in a twisted beech grove
of granite and lichen grays
for a night on a
platform bed hard by the double
oil barrel stove he welded. Listening,
Peter listening to the wind swarming
into the Minks from Kearsarge
bearing whatever messages it
chooses to share.

Vicky with Peter gone
spun more solidly
anchored more straightforward
more bold and independent by
necessity and inclination.
Without Peter's standards highest
Vicky charts her own,
singular and burnished
with her quiet brashness.

Torah portioned man
R'euven ben Ari, Reuben son of Lion
touching Torah
praying like a child not to
stumble fumble for blessing
that's me forty-five
child man older by two
than Rabbi Arnold.

Benjamin's off for three
year old Halloween
the red fox,
he was very specific,
but first
Doug, Marge, Jan, Roy, Vicky
come a ghosted trick
or treat and amaze
Wild-eyed he's scared
knowing but not knowing
that the people of the masks
and shrouds
have not
really changed.

Epiphanies or not
freedom or the sparkle of
skipping wisdom does not
relieve tumult and
Want
Want comes a-callin'
boredom or happiness pricked

want stretching from
scrotal entrenched desire,
wildlove making,
to fame's mirror kiss.
Fame's the collector's glee,
a possession in
meeting, knowing,
touching, avoiding—
I puff out a white-haired chest as
author, author, the dry.

Sex stage whispers through
memory of possibility,
reticence and surprise.
Fame is insatiable,
contesting with itself.
Sex is for itself
despite lust falling in.
Fame is history's glue,
the puffed mirror trick,
the armor over risk,
and self-appraisal.
Fame showers public opportunity
while it sucks away at truth
in the dazzle of applause,
the flow of cash
that's fame's cum.

Jan begins to cry in
the mall's baby section,
by paraphernalia we must have
but cannot begin even to name.
Stretching to the near horizon
in the rat's maze of boutiques,
video screens chattering,
I realize in its
dour sticky multiplicity
and nauseous wonder,
is the adults section.

Eight months
Jan's melon round,
still walking two miles
in the morning. Two hours
a Saturday. Slow down
says nurse-midwife
a-caring and I
decide no hope to rescue
my wreckage, to welcome
our son into life almost
as it is, as it may be.
Transformative dreams only
in a haze. Now
my piles of papers
no threat to
life's mystery fulfillment
of this impossible
world.

FIRST SNOW AGAIN,
in spite of cynicism,
suages November's
gray rage.
Destinies   Clinging to trees
the integument of water
of sky and ocean's blood.
Nature, the leveler
of birth and death
sorrow and joy
to adjectival exhaustion.

Birthdayed I am
From still point to chaos
spearing at truth
at life blinking between
the capacious clarity
of irresistible time
and confusion's cacophony.
Too romantic a bit
says Doug of my meditations.

But also as
unavoidable as
an apple falling,
a plunge that
marks
or mocks
the irrevocable.

Jennifer sweeps into
the laundromat from
a logger's day
wearing a pungent mist of
gasoline, bar and chain oil
pine pitch and wood chips.
Her arms are mottled
black with the marks of
exuberance, sweat and dirt.
Her jacket with an oil
skin coat, a soft stocking hat
crushed and broken
on her head. The
muscles of her arms
cord up as she flings
laundry into a dryer,
a down jacket with a boot
to fluff it dry. They own
no shoes. Samuel. Samuel.
Jennifer says annoyed when
I tell her my son's planned
name. Her Sam, she feels,
has unleashed a torrent of
epigenous imitation and forgery,
theft of her inventiveness.
Samuel, I assure her,
both my grandfathers' names
and meaning Shemu'el
asked of G-d, I say.

That will be it,
Shemu'el, she says
I'll call him Shemu'el,
and sweeps
out of the laundromat.

Fate is the arrow
that struck and
electrified itself,
unleashed the torrent
of destiny - placenta
amniotic sac and being.
Life rushing at us with
its forbearance and patience.
Spoken to, but not
reasoned to, in the swirl
that shreds our logic.

Doug's pigs slaughtered
a day of blood
and hot water and
hoists and guts and
warm, languid, heavy
bodies
hanging
cooling
for chops and hams and
sausages.
The country honesty and responsibility
of meat eaters.

Morality is in the killing
here. Killing assuaged
by the assertion of humane
practice or obliviousness
that connects slaughter house door
to plastic wrapped supermarket
body parts.

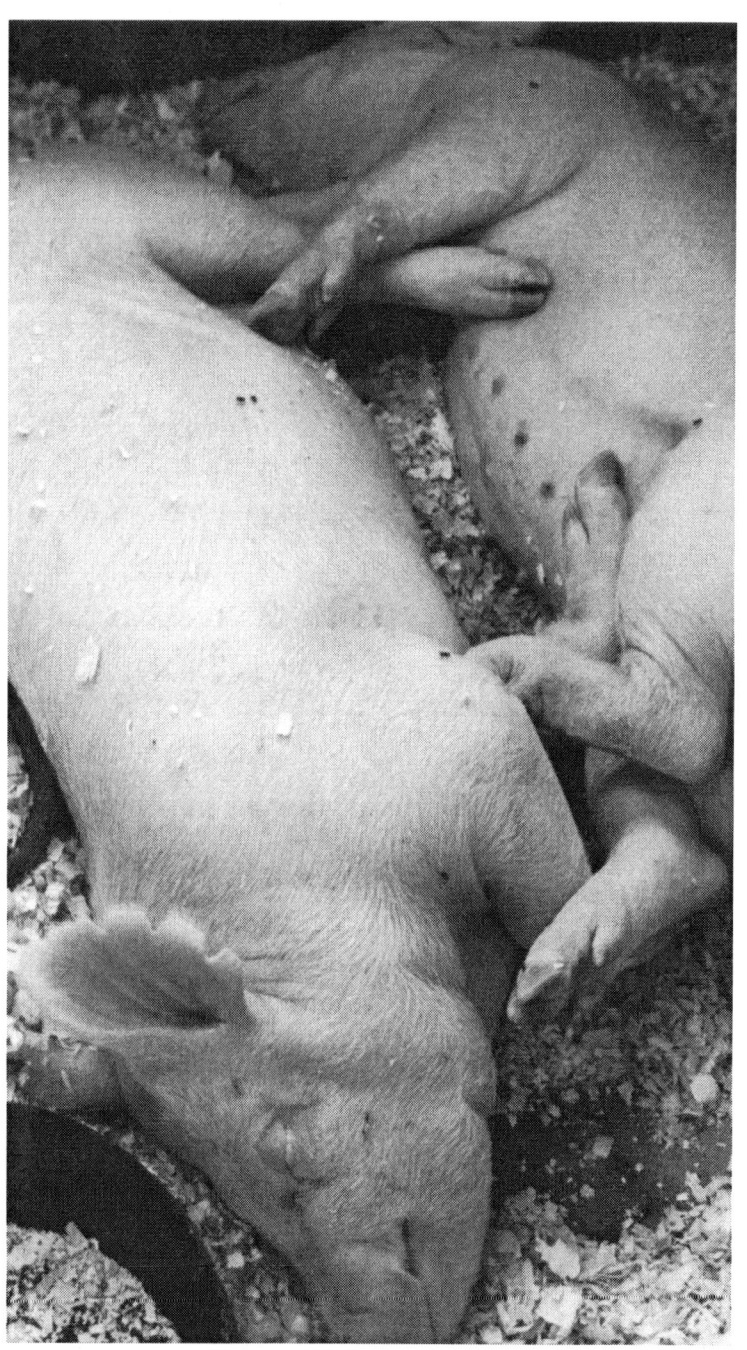

There's a farmer
whose pig next in line can watch
terror stricken the gutted carcass
of the pig before
spinning. It can be done
better, Doug says, a gentle
man's compassion for the
animals he'll kill to eat.
Not a meat eater,
I have nothing to say.
The other man's no factory farmer, but
pugnacious by reputation in his
farmer's struggle to survive
in a time of sub-divisions.

Benjamin has eaten his
first sausage made
from the meat of Harry,
an old friend.

Zero
Station

Zero degrees December night
snow creaks with the rasp of dry cold,
planets flash like lanterns,
the moon is convivial and full
tugging at the great and
small waters, the
night the midwife predicted
our baby our son to
be broken from
amniotic bliss.
Vicky practices breathing
with us a birth partner
intent on sharing
an incommensurable vicarious
thrill.

Oatmeal boiling
woodstove water whistling
due date falls away
into the confidence of
the after-time. Veterans
of pregnancy of adventuring
but not yet of birth,
of shallow kicks in the
belly but not the moans
coos and cries of a
child in the air.

Split in half
like the moon
by impending joy
we await
with bloody show
at zero station
lightening in the fervor
of terror masking
deliverance's exculpatory
exultation.
Emotions mixed a
cocktail of undrunk
liquors, a potion intoxicating and nameless.
Jan's turning inward,
lucid dreaming of stillness
of breath and silence
and moaned exclamation
of womb turned to rock
and the rock rumbling
pulsing laboring
of starts and stops
of motion that still
for now emits rest.

While she births a baby
I by her inspiration birth
in my own frantic
sympathetic aspiration,
in the shadow
of her wonder,
this poem of a book
and a tome of another.
Riding with her in the early
morning the three-thirty A.M.s
to shape, to finish,
to release.

A cold rain falls
melts snow to ice sheet,
uncovers winter's early riot
of brown and gray debris.
It's blue cohosh time
squaw root, they say
to speed and smooth
contractions rumbling.
The breathing exercises
seem a forgotten dream to me
This is unexplored territory.

Samuel

SAMUEL ARI ZOHAR SCHAFFER-MORRISON
blazing in Hanukkah night
lifted red and vernix burnished
from Jan's split belly.
Samuel, our son, in wonder   *Joy*
looming, rolling with
his ten pounds one ounce,
Samuel screaming into our time.
Samuel a universe renewed
December 19, 1992,
nineteen years after the night
Papa Sam, my grandfather, died.
Samuel of possibilities that
jade our industrial conceits
and humble vain words.
Our son mystery man,
of prospects unmeasured.
Murmurs of our first day,
I finger feed glucose
scrub meconium from his ass
and swollen testicles,
diaper, wrap him in a
receiving blanket
rock and stroke and comfort coo
our son birthed into a modernity
railing at its present, past
and prospect. Our son with
Jan's tight determined mouth.
Sculpted with my lips angled contours.
Separated, I tremble.

Flashes of fear and desire sizzle
mixing with exhaustion
spun with gratitude and
incipient tears of joy.
In Samuel's innocently willful
perfection he lies,
with all the young, as
the future of humanity
and its dominions, the shining
and copious beneficence of love.

Life's Leap

The company of women
enveloped Jan
Helped her labor
Stroked her head
Slid Samuel to
her breast
Took away her pain
and her urine.

The nursery of babies
resounds with
insistent desire,
calls of spring peepers the
exclamation of angry crows
swirling as part of the
chorus of infant loneliness
whose meaning is less pain
than stirring commencement
festooned with truth.

Morning of joy
and night of furies.
Reality is never a
tepid pool.

Compassion's elegy
for my son
sings a song
of utter need responsive
not to a vacant

universe wanting
but to personality's allure
that's not the trickster's pose
but the sign and
seed of consciousness,
life's leap to
mind and body
learning, loving.

Sam asleep
in wondrous rapture
along my chest
curled in heart's comfort
in memory of bliss
in warm respite
from exertion and
the universe's mysterious demands.

My father a man of few words
is evermore laconic.
A stopped down focus upon
the necessary, filled with
the nuance of the unsaid,
the pauses and spaces teeming
with concern.
About colic, he said,
through the lens of mind's eye
watching me wail,
"Put him over your
shoulder and pat his back."

Epilog

An elegy to simple deeds.

The woods still stand
in immemorial flux
over the kingdom of rock
winter and snow slung valley.
The heartening sound is not
the skidder's roar,
the saw's whine voracious,
but the deeper murmured buzzing
within these cold and gladed
hills, the friction, the
heat and light not of hitch
and metal and gasoline blunderbuss,
but the whirring of conversation
the turning and returning of generations
and not merely the machine thrusting,
the eating of soil and rock.
Glory not to the cutting,
but to the building.

Glory to the Building

In these folded hills
another generation rises
informed by parents' aspirations
passion and austere dreams,
where hope lies
in narrow rock-strewn crannies,
where wisdom races with the
irresistible spring melt down
Slaughter Brook to the Warner River
to the Contoocook and
to the once and soon again great Merrimack.
From the scars of our struggles unending
arises the glint in our children's eyes.

For beginnings unending.

G-d bless.

The author flailing dry beans for winnowing at Musterfield Farm Putting Up Day in Sutton N.H. "I am the bean man."

Roy Morrison lives in Warner N.H.

Glad Day Publishing Cooperative
(After an engraving by William Blake)

Book publishing is now in the hands of a few media conglomerates whose concern is not books, certainly not with literature or social change. With the elimination of independent bookstores and distribution through the chains the promotional lifetime of a book may now be measured in weeks.

There have always been small publishers aimed at a specialized readership. There have been recent technological breakthroughs in computerized desktop publishing and sophisticated promotion-distribution, allowing a minimum financial investment and small runs. Because of the crisis in mainstream publishing and with these advantages we have formed our own writers' publishing cooperative.

Our particular purpose is to bridge the gap between imaginative literature and political articles and criticism which have been fixed under the labels of "Fiction" and "Non-fiction." But the split has diminished literature and its usefulness to society. The hope of a literature that is positively useful has inspired us to call our publishing imprint GLAD DAY.

What has happened—even for those of us on the Left—is that there are three separated languages understood by separate readerships. Academic criticism. Protest and fact-finding journalism and exhortation. And "high culture" narrative fiction devoted to the deeper and complex themes reflected through individual characters and subjectivity. With these constraints writers find themselves engaged in self-censorship that has to do both with artistic and formal considerations and with what can be said. An exception is contemporary women's writing, which through pure zestfulness is allowed to be whole.

What has to be said by writers is that the present system is destructive of the earth and society and that the future it offers is not inevitable. And that this must be engaged by all literary means. In fact this has always been the tradition in literature.

The aim of GLAD DAY is the restoration of a political literature. Members of our writers' editorial collective have no other criteria than this and hold diverse views.